STORIES OF ROME

LUCUMO

SAM VANDERPLAS

LUCERNA

This edition published in 2025 by Lucerna Press
Fort Worth, Texas

This work was developed with the assistance of artificial intelligence
tools. The content reflects the author's intent and judgment.

ISBN: 979-8-9994863-0-1

Printed in the United States of America

STORIES OF ROME

LUCUMO

ADAPTED FROM LIVY

SAM VANDERPLAS

LUCERNA

Lucumo lived in Tarquinii,
a proud and ancient city of Etruria.
Its temples were old, its customs older still,
and its people took pride in both.

His father had come from Corinth,
a Greek exile driven from his homeland.
He crossed the sea
seeking refuge among strangers.

He settled in Tarquinii,
learned the language, and kept the peace.
In time, he married a noblewoman,
a daughter of a leading house.

From this union came Lucumo—
born of a foreign father and Etruscan mother,
rich in blood and gold,
but not truly at home in either land.

Lucumo grew tall and capable.
He inherited land, horses, and treasure.
He honored the gods of Etruria
and kept the customs of his mother's house.

But the men of Tarquinii did not forget.
They called him the son of a foreigner.
They praised his wealth,
but denied him honor.

He could not serve in public office.
He was not counted among the citizens.
His words were measured,
but never invited.

He walked among them as one tolerated,
never as one accepted.
And so he turned his thoughts southward—
to a city still young, where a man might rise.

His wife, Tanaquil, was learned in omens and
firm in counsel.
She spoke what both of them knew.
"The city is closed to you," she said.
"You will never be more than a stranger here."

"Let us go to Rome," she told him.
"There, men rise by merit, not birth."
Lucumo listened and did not argue.
She had read the signs and spoken truly.

They gathered their goods,
called the servants,
loaded the carts,
and did not look back.

With no promise of welcome,
they entered the open road.

The road passed shrines and boundary
stones.
Lucumo rode in silence, hand on the reins.
Their household followed behind him,
drawn by oxen.

The land grew flatter.
The sky stretched wider.
The winds were different here,
and the road more worn.

Lucumo had no friends in Rome.
He bore no Roman name.
But he had gold, horses, and will.
And he sought a place to be known.

He left behind a proud city that scorned him.
He looked toward a rough city that might
receive him.
And the road went on beneath the sun,
leading them to the gates of Rome.

As they approached the city,
an eagle appeared overhead—
suspended on her wings,
gently stooping from the sky.

With swift precision,
she took the cap from Lucumo's head.
Then, flying round the cart with loud
screams,
she circled as if sent from heaven for the
purpose.

All stood still.
Even the oxen halted on the road.
The cap was not dropped.
No one spoke.

Then the eagle descended once more,
orderly replaced the cap upon his head,
and rose aloft,
vanishing into the sky.

Tanaquil received the omen with great joy.
She was skilled in the signs of the heavens,
as the Etruscans are known to be,
and she understood what had been shown.

She embraced her husband and said,
"This eagle was sent by Jupiter.
It came from the heights of the sky,
a messenger of the king of gods."

"It flew about the highest part of your body,
and took its covering—
not to steal it,
but to restore it by divine command."

"Hope for great things," she said.
"The gods have marked you for a crown."

Rome was smaller than Tarquinii,
rougher, louder, crowded with strangers.
Its houses were wood and clay.
Its streets were uneven and alive.

But the gates stood open.
And no man questioned their coming.
Latin farmers called out in the market,
Sabine herdsmen crossed the Tiber.

Etruscans, Latins, and Sabines all walked its
roads.
No one asked Lucumo where he came from.
No one mocked his name.
He passed as any other man.

In a city of many tongues and many gods,
there was room for him.
So he made his home in Rome,
and waited to be known.

Lucumo gained favor through gracious
speech.
He welcomed guests with food and honor.
He praised men of rank and influence,
and gave gifts that would not be forgotten.

He sought friends by kindness and boldness.
He honored those who might lift him higher.
He gave where it would bear fruit,
and waited.

The Romans began to call him Tarquinius,
after the city he had left behind.
He did not correct them.
He wore the name lightly.

He had no tribe and no lineage.
But he worked carefully to win a place.
And the people approved
what they believed he had earned.

Merchants spoke of him in the forum.
Laborers repeated his words.
Artisans praised his generosity.
Even children knew his name.

The king heard of him.
Ancus Marcius ruled with prudence.
He asked who this stranger was
whom the people admired.

He was told of the man from Tarquinii—
a foreigner who spoke with tact,
gave with purpose,
and won men's favor without demanding it.

The king said, "Let him come."
And word was sent.
The stranger would be brought
to stand before the king.

Tarquinius came without fear.
He bowed low and spoke plainly.
He asked for nothing,
and he gave no boast.

The king listened with care.
He saw wisdom in his speech,
strength in his bearing,
and restraint in his words.

He invited him to return.
Tarquinius came again,
and again after that,
until he was expected.

What began as a single meeting
became friendship.
And the king kept him near,
as a man to be trusted.

The king summoned him to council.
Tarquinius listened more than he spoke.
He advised in disputes,
in treaties, and in law.

He learned the customs of the city.
He obeyed the ancient rites.
He was present at sacrifices,
and careful in judgment.

He was no longer a stranger.
He was seen beside the king in public and in
private.
His voice was heard among Roman elders.
His name was known in every quarter.

The king gave him charge of many affairs.
He was sent to speak for Rome in foreign
towns.
He oversaw laborers on public works.
He gave counsel in matters of peace and war.

He carried messages with care,
and returned with honest report.
He kept accounts, settled quarrels,
and made ready what the king required.

In each task he was tested.
In each duty he proved faithful.
The king found no fault in him,
and trusted him with greater things.

He gave freely to those in need,
and welcomed many into his home.
He remembered names, returned kindness,
and carried himself as one who belonged.

His gifts were well chosen.
His words won goodwill.
None could say what he sought—
only that he served the city well.

Though not born among them,
they called him their own.
And his name was honored in every quarter.

The king had watched him closely.
In each matter, Tarquinius had spoken wisely.
In each task, he had acted without fault.
In peace and in trouble, he had proved steady.

He had been sent on embassies.
He had overseen public works.
He had advised in matters of war and
judgment.
He had never broken faith.

He stood beside the king
in counsel and in ceremony.
His voice was known among the elders.
His name was spoken with care.

And being now proven in every trust,
and found faithful in all things,
he was at length, by the king's will,
appointed guardian to his children …

Archaeological Echoes: The Ara della Regina

The Ara della Regina ("Altar of the Queen"), below, is the largest and most important Etruscan temple yet discovered, standing on a plateau in modern Tarquinia—the site of ancient Tarquinii. Built around the 5th century BC, the temple had stood for generations by the time Lucumo journeyed to Rome. Its grand size and elaborate terracotta decorations reveal the wealth and artistic sophistication of Tarquinii, one of the leading cities of Etruria. The foundations are still visible today. The temple once rose with tall wooden columns and a broad roofline, crowned by striking sculptures.